Finding God Without Religion:

A

Pathway To Inner Peace

And

Inner Joy

By: Ibikunle Fayemi

Published by:

Ibikunle Fayemi

5, Tijani Bello Street, Ojodu-Ikeja, Lagos, South-West Nigeria.

+2348127718107 and +2348033511207

Copyright © Ibikunle Fayemi 2018

ISBN: 9781983203671

APPRECIATION

I will like to thank my brother, Adeniyi Fayemi, who sent me the two books that opened my eyes to authentic spirituality. May you too always enjoy the simple pleasures that life has to offer.

DEDICATION

This book is dedicated to my inner guide, "Something That Speaks But Is Not Seen. It continues to teach and thrill.

TABLE OF CONTENT

INTRODUCTION

You believe there is a "God". And your faith in "God" is unshakeable. But, every time you say "God" said this, "God" said that, you are actually repeating what you read in books or what someone else told you. If the above applies to you, then, this book is for you. This book is not about beliefs. It is about the writer's inner experience. It deals with the possibility of communicating with something that is not seen but speaks. It deals with taking a plunge into the abyss of human thoughts to explore the non-observable human psychological landscape. It deals with the writer finding inner peace and inner joy by simply following the inner prescription of "striving to do the right things the right way". If you have a thirst for knowledge, this book is for you. It may set you on your own path towards contentment and fulfillment.

Let us assume that I tell you that certain door is locked. And, because you believe me, you do not attempt to open that door. That door will remain locked in your mind. And you will never know if that door is open or not, because you, and your mind, have believed that the door is locked. And, for all practical purposes, it will no longer make sense for you to use that door as an exit. Meanwhile, the door is not locked in concrete reality. I have simply misinformed you. But your belief has locked that door in your subjective reality.

It is clear from the above that your belief that the door is locked is a false belief. It is not true because it has misinformation as its foundation. However, a modern human invention called the "scientific method" mandates that we verify all things. And a verse in the bible also advises that one should "test all things".

It is imperative that any mind that wants to call itself modern must "install" the scientific method into his, her mind. If not, delusion, which is simply false belief, will infiltrate that mind and make it susceptible to superstition. I have met people that are naturally intelligent, yet whose beliefs limit their thoughts. And consequently, they could not grow intellectually, mentally, beyond those beliefs. Did I just describe one of the recipes of stagnation? Stagnation is the name of the disease that stops one from changing what is not working. The cure? Creativity. This is simply the ability to replace old, familiar pattern of living with a new, better one.

Innovation. "Innovation is defined simply as a "new idea, device, or method." "Innovation distinguishes a leader from a follower"... Steve Jobs

"Every positive change in your life begins with a clear, unequivocal decision that you are going to either do something or stop doing something." ~Brian Tracy. I had thoughts in my head that begged for expression. However, I could not freely express myself in front of my elders because these thoughts diverge from my elders' thoughts. So I fled from the presence of my elders. And I became free. Now, I am my own man, a wholesome man, complete, unencumbered by ancient thoughts. My thoughts, my acts, and my life are now in perfect alignment. "Happiness is when what you think, what you say, and what you do are in harmony." Mahatma Gandhi. Try to discover yourself. You may find inner joy, inner peace, along the way, like I did, twenty two years ago.

Treating others the way we want to be treated is said to be the Golden Rule. It is fairness. It is doing the right things the right way. The core of the messages of all religions is: "Do unto others as you want done unto you." If we all abide by this principle as the essence of "God," we will not go wrong. This is one of the prerequisites for entering the 'kingdom of God" within.

Mental models are deeply ingrained assumptions and generalizations that influence how we understand the world. Majority calls it beliefs. Until these are brought to the surface and thoroughly scrutinized, little knowledge takes place that does not conform to these models. I have since discovered that my thinking controls my emotions. Consequently, I chose the thinking that creates pleasant feelings over the one that creates the unpleasant ones. Overall, the chosen thoughts must be truthful, mostly peaceful, or else, disappointment, frustration, and anger, the natural enemies of happiness, will seep into one's reality. Everyday can be a good day if we so desire. Everyday can be a fulfilling day if only we can accept that some inevitable things cannot be avoided. Illness will afflict. Death will come. And burial will follow. These are simply part of life. My father's death in 2012 was on a good day. The money in my pocket added to the goodness of that day. His burial the next day, according to my desire, was a fulfilling day, regardless of the sweet tears of joy that dropped from my eyes. I was happy that I was able to bury him and not vice versa. Most times, it is not what happens to us or done to us that hurt us. What hurt us is actually how we respond. And how we respond is largely determined by how we think, or what we believe. And we are ultimately responsible for choosing the kind of thoughts that make everyday a good, fulfilling day. I have made my choice. And may I continue to reap its benefits tomorrow, just like I did yesterday and today. Life is good. And, life is sweet.

Who is richer between a man that has little, yet content with what he has, and a man that has much, but afflicted with discontent? The contented man with little is psychologically richer than the discontented man with much. While the former feeds his soul, the latter feeds his ego. There is nothing beyond satisfaction but greed. Greed is bad. Curb it. One of her child is corruption, a cog in the wheel of spiritual/psychological growth.

I may be non-religious but definitely not anti-religion. A mystic cannot be anti-religion. My non-religious status is strategic. My neutrality guarantees impartiality towards all religions. There is no reason for me to defend or attack any religion unjustly. And I do not dance to the tune of any foreign ideology. Therefore, any time I find myself in disagreement with anyone who is "truly" religious, and not the ostentatious one, of which we have many, there is need to go back to the "Source" for clarification. Universal truths are never in conflict unless some kind of corruption has occurred.

If a blind man says he cannot see anything, he is right. But if he proceeds to assert that because he sees nothing, there is nothing, it would come across as enforcing his reality on others who do not share his limitation. We ought to refrain from trying to impose our limitations on other who do not share our limitations. We are all not on the same level of mental/spiritual/psychological development.

CHAPTER 1

THE INWARD JOURNEY

Inward Journey is about inner experience. It deals with the possibility of communicating with something that is not seen but speaks. It is about taking a plunge into the abyss of human thoughts to explore the non-observable human psychological landscape. One of the gains of this exploration is bringing to light ideas that are new and useful. It deals with finding inner peace and inner joy. A vehicle for this journey is meditation, a breathing exercise with a focus on in and out breathing.

I had never heard of "Inward Journey" until 1996. So, there was no way I could have consciously decided to embark on any inward journey that I had never heard of. My own inward journey started unwittingly. I was at life's dead end. My life was in shambles, ruined. But instead of giving up, I decided to give living a clean lifestyle a chance. I vowed not to get involved in any form of illegality again. I began to retrain myself. I took a correspondence course in Short Story Writing and Journalism. I also obtained a bachelors and masters degrees, all in business administration.

The voice surfaced after the writing course. And it served as a guide in my rehabilitation. About a week after the voice surfaced, I could not sleep well. I was very miserable. Depression took the thrill, the joy, the sweetness out of my life. Things that I had done in the past, some that I could not consciously remember, came to my mind. The consequences of those things I have done also came to my mind. They joined together like siamese twin. Amazing. It was like watching a movie to see its climax. I obtain my knowledge that "I always reap what I sow" from this inner experience. That was when it dawn on me that I was the one, through my thinking, my actions, my relationship with others, that manufactured my negative consequences. Upon that realization, like a fog, the misery lifted, leaving in its wake my customary inner joy and peace. That was when I vowed to always strive to do the right things, the right way, at all times, in all things.

The voice said he was "God". And, because I was hearing a male voice, I automatically assumed "God" was male. But the voice corrected me that I should not assume that the shape of water in a cup is the shape of water. The voice asked me where he was. I confidently replied that he was inside my head. Then the voice told me to turn on the radio and a female voice filled the room. Then voice asked me if the woman talking on the radio was inside the radio. I knew the woman was not inside the radio. I knew she was at a studio somewhere else. I knew it was the radio wave, via a transmitter and a receiver that brought the female voice into my room. I was no longer confident in my knowledge that the voice is actually inside my head or if I was just hearing it inside my head.

The first time I heard the "voice" inside my head, I told my younger brother. And my brother, without verification, said "Ah! That's our mother's voice you are hearing. "Imagine that. He was wrong. I was actually hearing a silent, male "voice." I was in an uncharted psychological landscape, unknown to my brother and unknown to many. But, with time, with verification, and of course with experience, I knew the "voice" I was hearing inside my head. I was hearing the voice of reasoning. I was hearing the voice of "God". I was hearing a "voice" that constantly compels me to do the right things the right way, in all things and at all times.

Now, my own "God" is inside my head. My own "God" speaks directly to me inside my head, not through a third party. Yes, I admit to hearing a voice inside my head. That is why I said I have evolved into a mystic, modern, pragmatic, but mystic nonetheless. If you think I am mad, wait till you hear this: The people that wrote the books majority calls the "word of God" claimed to hear a voice too. Then what?

Of Objective and Subjective Reality.

If something exists in your head but not in the world you share with others, then, it is subjective reality. It could be true, for you, but not for others, at least, not yet. You may be a visionary. Or it could be delusional, a false belief you carry in your head, maybe for self-esteem purposes, or for entertainment at best. If it does not exist in your head, but exist in the world you share with others, in objective reality, you could be ignorant, but not averse to learning. Or, you are mentally blind. And you can be a menace to society. You can easily injure yourself or injure other people with your mental blindness. If it exist in your head and it also exist in the world you share with others, in both subjective reality and objective reality, then, you are spiritually/psychologically aligned, ready to embrace lasting success and enduring happiness.

I see a lot of people wrestling with archaic knowledge that neither describes their present terrain, nor solves their pertinent problems. And, no amount of persuasion can make them bulge from the quagmire they have found themselves in. They will insist they are right, that they are simply following either their culture, or their religion. It would not have been a tragedy if they are living a satisfying, fulfilling lifestyle. Far from it. Their lives are full of privation, of discomfort, of begging just to keep body and soul together.

It would have been better if they were ignorant, vacuous. It would have been a delight to train, educate them. But they are not ignorant per se. They have been miseducated with knowledge that is no longer relevant, pertinent. And they are not intelligent enough to realize the obsoleteness of their so-called knowledge. Regardless of all their religious observance, if they do not have the love of truth, "God" will continue to send them a strong dosage of delusion, and they will continue to believe lies. Believing lies and acting on them waste time, efforts, with no favorable results. Because the mind does not have the capacity to know what is true or not, it is the responsibility of lovers of truth to test all things to ascertain their veracity before stamping anything as true. The truth always works. If most things are working well in your life, that is good for you. That is the clearest sign that you have mitigated delusion.

CHAPTER 2

THE REAL DEAL

The sole purpose of going to school is to get educated, not just to get a certificate. The certificate is just to confirm that one attended certain school. It is also to confirm that one finished from that school. However, we are all aware that it is possible for one to obtain a certificate without being properly educated.

Using the same analogy, the sole purpose of going to religious houses is to become spiritual, not just to become religious. The attendance at the religious houses is just to confirm that one is receiving instruction on how to become spiritual. However, we know it is possible to attend regular service at religious houses without becoming spiritual. I am using the word "spiritual" here to mean "going beyond the seen into the unseen for the sole purpose of obtaining spiritual guidance."

After graduating from school, one will naturally go into the world, in search of job. It is on the job that the adequacy, the effectiveness of one's education will be verified.

Same thing ought to apply to the one attending services at religious houses. Naturally, when he goes out to mingle in the world, his behavior ought to confirm the glorious instructions he has been consuming from his/her preferred religious house. Is he humble? Is he just? Does he love? Is he successful? Is he happy? Is he upright, and therefore, not corrupt? Does he do the right things the right way even if no one is looking?

The final analysis is this: The quality of productivity and efficiency should be use in determining who is truly versed in the art of living. Fruits, ladies and gentlemen, fruits are the ultimate verification of what type a tree is.

A lot of people do not know what "God" is. And, this ignorance shows in the unsatisfactory life they are living. As someone who has evolved into a mystic, I know it is possible to have a two-way communication with "God" without being schizophrenic. This two-way communication is what provides authentic spiritual guidance, and not the noise making one-way communication presently going on with the people you will think ought to know better.

In an attempt to communicate with "God", these people make so much noise. And consequently, they disturb the peace and tranquility of other people. It is an ethical axiom that our rights stop where other people's right begin. Yes, the noise-makers in the guise of worshipping "God" have a right of worship, but so do others have a right to their peace and tranquility. If I were them, I will heed the advice once given that they should go inside their rooms, where no one can neither see nor hear them whenever they want to pray. Doing the right things the right way has no substitute. Also, as a mystic, I am aware of a "God" that can read minds, that can speak in a silent voice. A voice so silent it will be drowned in the cacophony of noise making some people mistaken for prayer.

A lot of people are not making that much progress because they have become rigid in their thinking, and consequently stagnant in their progress. They have lost the ability to interpret reality effectively. I think accurate interpretation of reality is fundamental to all human progress. And clarity of mind, not prejudice, is needed to interpret reality effectively. However, clarity of mind may elude any mind burning with anger, hatred, and greed.

Some people have mastered "God" and all that is in heaven. I have not. But I have mastered how to live a fulfilling life, with more or with less…, outside of Nigeria and in Nigeria, with corruption, and without corruption.

The following is a parable: If you claim that you have access to plenty water, why is that unwanted fire is still burning under your rooftop? You keep bragging about your unlimited access to, not just water, but the cleanest, yet, the fire is still burning. Your water is better than his, cleaner than his, you keep saying. Yet, the fire under your rooftop is still burning. Is it not the smoke from it, the smoke of discomfort, of disappointment, of dejection wafting up to the sky for all to see? Look very well. His water that you called dirty has quenched his unwanted fire. It is no longer burning. He is at peace with himself because he has peace under his rooftop. Hey, who cares about your water that you called the cleanest when it could not quench the unwanted fire under your own rooftop? Ideals are good. But practicality is what always matters. And the usefulness of water, whether clean or dirty, in this case, should be the effectiveness of it in quenching unwanted fire, either under one's rooftop, or the rooftops of friends and family.

Every human has innate strengths, raw talents. But it has to be developed either through proper upbringing or self-development. But some people have been classically conditioned to think that they cannot do what they have the potential to do. Ultimately, they have learned how to be helpless. This is called "Learned Helplessness." What Is Learned Helplessness? "Learned helplessness occurs when an animal is repeatedly subjected to an aversive stimulus that it cannot escape. Eventually, the animal will stop trying to avoid the stimulus and behave as if it is utterly helpless to change the situation. Even when opportunities to escape are presented, this learned helplessness will prevent any action. While the concept is strongly tied to animal psychology and behavior, it can also apply to many situations involving human beings. When people feel that they have no control over their situation, they may also begin to behave in a helpless manner. This inaction can lead people to overlook opportunities for relief or change." By Kendra Cherry

Those who know how to learn, and want to learn, will continuously use their innate intelligence to acquire pertinent knowledge, either by critical thinking/reasoning, research, or simply listening to those that already knows. If your culture or religion has taught you how to be helpless, it is time to break free of that "learned helplessness" and replace it with "can do" attitude.

When someone walks in the center of "God's" will, his/her steps will be ordered. How do we know "God's"? Will? We have so many custodians of "God's" will. But we can use reverse reasoning to arrive at what many may regard as true. If it is true that if someone walks in the center of "God's" will, his/ steps will be ordered, then it will also be true that someone with ordered steps is walking in the center of "God's" will. By seeing his/her ordered life, and not one in disarray, we will know that someone is walking in the center of "God's" will. Not so? The fruits are the best indicator of what type a tree is. Therefore, wanting an ordered life is not something to pray for. It ought to be a desire, backed up by striving to do the right things the right way, if not in all things, in most things, if not all the time, most of the time. It is everyone that will carry his/her own cross. And, a sick man that keeps taking fake drugs may never get well.

CHAPTER 3
SOMETHING THAT SPEAKS BUT IS NOT SEEN

Is there something called "God?" Can a two-way communication take place between humans and "God"? Does "Something that Speaks but is Not Seen" resides in the human minds? Can one know his/her purpose in life? Is it possible to harness dreams to a point that they become fertile source of creativity?

I have explored all these and much more with meditation. I have moved beyond beliefs into the realm of knowing. The concept of "God" can be explored within modern context, without importation of ideology, without tall tales of antiquity, with the aim of fostering creativity.

I may like or not like what others say "God" is. But I cannot dispute what they say. I do not have enough experiential knowledge to do that. In my opinion "God" is unknowable. The answer I got to the question, "What is God?" from my probing in meditation was, "God is unknowable. But some of (his?) (Its?) Manifestations that may be unknown at some point in time can be made known by those that are spiritually/mentally awakened." From that point onward, I stopped confusing "the man pointing to the moon for the moon." I simply listen, in silence, to "Something that speaks but is not seen", a silent voice in my abyss of thoughts. A voice that thrills, taunts, teaches. I subject all thoughts from this source to the verification process while not ignoring a caveat that came from the same source that, "Ideals are good but practicality is what always matters."

I embarked on an "inward journey" in 1996. I wanted to know "What is God", among other things. The journey is still ongoing. And, the answer I got to the question, in 1997, was "God is unknowable. But some of his manifestations can be made known by the mentally or spiritually awakened ones." This is the totality of my knowledge about what "God" is.

I do not argue the existence or non-existence of "God". I leave that for the "experts", which a lot of people are anyway. My focus is on actions/inactions and corresponding verifiable results. I am not moved by mere claims. I have to see the manifestation of the Real Thing in the quality of life people are living.

As a pragmatic mystic, I only focus on the practicality of the idea. I neither gain nor lose by arguing for or against "God" concepts. What is it that I can do or gain by shouting on top of my lungs that "God exist? You must believe as I believe!" The people that did so, or continue to do so, did it, are doing it to dominate, to colonize. What is my own whether you believe in one "God" or many "Gods" or not? What competitive advantage do I gain apart from the domination and colonization that I already mentioned? And I am neither into domination nor colonization. My motivation is fueled by the desire to ignite my compatriots' critical, creative, and innovative thinking ability so that we can unshackle our archaic, colonized minds.

I wish we can be humble enough to know that we do not truly know what or who "God" is. Simply repeating what we have read, or what some other people told us about "God" may not true knowledge. And until we admit that, we all will be wallowing in our mental arrogance of thinking we know what we may truly not know. How come there is an inverse correlation between some people's knowledge of "God" and production/progress if they truly know what and who "God" is? Those who know better do better.
Once the humility to admit triumphed over the arrogance, the tyranny of certainty, we may all realize, like I did as a mystic, that what we are actually wrestling with are ideas about "God." These

ideas may be true or false or may be good or bad. Ideas that may have the seed of mediocrity in it or that may have potential for excellence. And, like St. Augustine said, "Faith is to believe what you do not see; the reward of this faith is to see what you believe.'

Like I said earlier, a lot of people know what/who "God" is, with certainty. I do not. I approach the concept of God with ignorance, with curiosity, with open mind. They approach it with beliefs they have elevated to the level of knowledge. And, consequently, suffer from tyranny of certainty. I am a knower who relies heavily on observation, experience, reasoning, logic and verification.

The more I try to explain myself to some people, to make them realize I may be different from them, the more they are resisting understanding me because I do not fit into their belief system, which, unfortunately, has become their prejudice. Clarity, thus, continues to elude them. And some people still wonder why bad things happen to "good" people? Prejudice! Prejudice, the act of prejudging people is bad. Be aware. Desist. And, get a cure by cultivating a beginner's mind. What is labeled "beginner's mind" here has since evolved into "learning mode". A "beginner's mind" "refers to having an attitude of openness, eagerness, and lack of preconceptions when studying a subject, even when studying at an advanced level, just as a beginner in that subject would." In addition, instead of prejudice, a lot of people need to develop empathic listening skills. "Empathic listening (also called active listening or reflective listening) is a way of listening and responding to another person that improves mutual understanding and trust." Anyone that wants to gain clarity must begin by striving to do the right things the right way. No effective decision can be made without clarity. And, decisions made without clarity always lead to frustration, dejection, unfulfillment.

Mahalia Jackson, an American gospel singer, wrote the following. And I passionately agree with her. "We must demonstrate what we know about God in the way we think, talk, walk, and live. God is peace. God is strength. God is mercy. God is forgiving. God is all knowing, all powerful, abundant, radiant life. God is Love. To know God is to be like Him. All else is a figment of y(our) imagination." A lot of people descended to the depth where lies are more comforting than truths. They need to soar to the height where truths are more comforting than lies. How do we know the truths? They work... even if not on the short run... on the long run. "Faith is to believe what you do not see; the reward of this faith is to see what you believe.' St. Augustine. Is our faith manifesting in our lives? Or is it just lifeless ideas to be debated with people of other faith, or nonbelievers?

We all know that there is relative order in the universe. Let us assume that this order is a manifestation of "God." So, anyone who claims to have knowledge of "God", or has a relationship with Him, must naturally have order in his or her life. Order, which is now the fruit, is how we can tell the tree, which is the knowledge of "God," or a relationship with Him. And for me, once anyone has the fruit, whether he/she believes in "God" or not, I automatically know that he/she has done the right things the right way. Or else the fruit won't be his/hers. Ordered thinking is a prerequisite for ordered life. Dwelling on mere tree when one already has the favorable and desirable fruit is unprogressive.

The first step towards creating order is self-discipline, self-control, self denial, coupled with "let your yes be yes, and let your no be no." When we have disciplined ourselves up to the point where "doing the right things the right way" becomes second nature, creating order, even in the midst of chaos, in our lives becomes inevitable. Order, whether created and sustained with peace, love and justice, or created and sustained with almighty power, is still order. But I personally prefer the one created and sustained with peace, love, and justice.

We all know that all sort of fraudsters use the name of "God," mostly in vain, in contravention of one of the 10 Commandments. Alarm in my head goes off when people use the name of "God" where it is not necessary. I become more cautious.

For example: If I ask a mechanic if he knows what is wrong with my car and he says, Olorun a ko wa mo se, (God will teach us how to do it) I know I am in for a ride of trial and error. Attaching the name of "God" to incompetence does not produce competence. Attaching the name of "God" to corrupt proceeds is a crude attempt to show authentic blessing via the fruits of the spirits.

Focused studies, coupled with disciplined practice, is what brings competence to life. Doing the right things the right way is the only path to righteousness, uprightness, not the unscrupulous attachment of "God's" name to irrelevance. Be warned.

The clearest sign to know who has "God" in his/her life is the manifestation of the "fruits of the spirits" in that person's life. And the clearest sign that one is seeking "God" is a lifestyle that reeks of uprightness, a lifestyle that is infused with diligence. It was true that one can tell a tree by the fruits it bears. It is still true now. And, it was true that the manifestation of Love is the presence of "God". It is still true now. A lifestyle of corruption, of hating on others, is not compatible with "God".

I constructively criticize religion, not antagonize it. All religions are supposedly rooted in righteousness. And as a mystic, I must embrace righteousness, and abstain from all form of evil. If you see my constructive criticism as negative, check yourself, constructively. You may be a negative person cloaking yourself as a religious person. Or...you may either be sincerely wrong, or zealously misguided.

The proliferation of "adulterated doctrines" in our midst is a manifestation of corruption. Corruption and uprightness are not compatible. If you like pray ceaselessly and fast for two hundred days. At least the rest of us will have enough to eat by your abstinence.

I am for the type of religion that fused rights and obligations together. As a pragmatic mystic, it is pleasant to my soul. It is the delusional type that proclaims rights but disdains obligations that I find odious.

How can you come to me, bragging about "God's" promises to you when you are clearly failing in upholding His commandments?
Religious beliefs, without uprightness is like a car without engine. It will take you nowhere but keep you in one spot. Or why do you think a lot of people fail to live satisfying lives? That nagging, persistent feeling of inadequacy is a clear sign of spiritual malnourishment. Change your ways.

Spiritual growth requires that we go beyond books, beyond the known, into the realm of unknown, if we desire to push the frontier of civilization towards growth, towards enduring happiness and lasting success. If we do otherwise, we will stagnate.

In December of 2016, I asked the following question: Does "God" really care who suffers and who doesn't? I could not answer this question at that time. But I think I can answer that question now: It is not for "God" to care who suffers and who does not. It is for the individual to use his/her dominion over most things to make sure he or she does not suffer, by doing the right things the right way.

Quite a lot of people have said, are saying, "God" works in mysterious ways." Yes, that may be technically true. But we have to work, diligently, ceaselessly, to unravel that mystery. If we do not, we will continue to live in ignorance, in perpetual backwardness.

The definition of mystery is "something that is difficult or impossible to understand." And, the definition of ignorance is "lack of knowledge or information." Spot the difference? Is mystery not synonymous with ignorance? Is unraveling mystery not the fulcrum on which modern knowledge turns?

Beliefs and life experience ought to match. If they do not, then we may be lying to ourselves. Your beliefs or non-beliefs about "God" have no relevance to me. It does not produce any verifiable competitive advantage. However, you doing the right things, the right way, in all things, and at all times, regardless of your beliefs or non-beliefs about "God," that is what is sacrosanct to me. The "fruits" are still the best way for me to tell whether the "tree" is fertile or barren.

CHAPTER 4
WHAT IS MYSTIC?

In the first chapter, I called myself a mystic. I know a lot of people may not know what a mystic is. First of all, let me define what mysticism is. Mysticism is the belief in the possibility of attaining direct communion with Ultimate Reality or knowledge of spiritual truths as by meditation.

However, for me, this is no longer a belief. It is now an experience. I sparingly use beliefs these days. A mystic is one who professes to undergo profound spiritual experiences. I began to tag myself as a mystic when a silent voice surfaced in my mental realm and began to teach and guide me. It was the voice that introduced me to the idea of verification, even before I studied the scientific method.

What is a Modern Mystic? A modern mystic is a mystic who applies the scientific method to his or her spiritual experiences and thereby produces useful practical knowledge that has applicability in concrete reality. A modern mystic, by extension, is also a pragmatic mystic. This is why I always insist that I must prove, verify all things. It is also the reason why I declared that "ideals are good but practicality is what always matters." In relating to me, forget what you have read in books about mysticism. I have forgotten all I read about it. I only use what I have experienced, the part that is practical, the part that has added value, spice to my life.

It is very clear to me that I have a system that works, relatively, for me.
I do not covet other people's system. And neither do I import that of others. Think of me as being spiritually independent and interdependent. After my inculcated beliefs system collapsed, I began to painstakingly rebuild another one. I relied heavily on experiences, observations, reasoning, and verifications. Of course I had help. There is that silent voice in the abyss of my thoughts that always teaches, thrills, taunts. Yes, sometimes it taught. Sometimes it thrilled. And sometimes it taunted. But it ultimately guided me away from my corrupt ways by steering me towards striving to do the right things the right way, in most things, and if not at all times, most of the time.

Is this inspiration, revelation, or divination? It does not matter your choice of word. One thing that is certain is: It is spiritual guidance. Yes, you can call it whatever you want. It does not really matter to me. After all, a rose called by any name will still smell the same way. It is still teaching, thrilling, and taunting when the need calls for it. Why do you think I continue to live, love and laugh? I

am not hurting. I do not hate. I am healed. And I continue to enjoy
the simple pleasures of life.

The following is a poem I wrote describing this voice in my abyss
of thought.

Union.

It comes. It helps.
Does it plan to stay?
If it stays,
that will be good.
If it leaves,
it will be missed.
It spreads love.
It tells the truth.
It is fair, and
it makes me laugh.
It thrills, it teaches.
Sometimes it taunts.
It makes friend with Time.
It milks Time
for all Time's worth.
It always speaks

with a silent voice.
A silent voice
only I can hear.
Sometimes it is not working,
It takes a break, then,
a pen feels like a shovel,
a blank paper looks like an
unploughed piece of land.
The well of thoughts
runs dry. And I wait,
and wonder and ponder.
Then it comes.

I had a dream in 1979, thirty nine years ago. And I still remember it vividly as if it was yesterday. It is one of those dreams that stay fresh in your mind, that one is unable to forget.

In that dream, I was supposed to go and speak to my father. But I must go through two men who were manning the gate to his house. On getting to his house, the two men manning the gate were busy arguing passionately and were unaware that I was around. I slipped pass them, went into my father's room, spoke to him and he spoke to me.

The next morning, my grandfather woke me up from my dream around 6:00am for the mandatory morning prayers. I had gone to Sagamu, Ogun State, Nigeria to spend my two weeks annual vacation from Nigerian Airways where I was working at the time. I woke up quite alright but I did not get up. I simply told my grandfather that I was not a Christian anymore. The old man could not believe his ears. So he repeated himself and I repeated myself. Then what I said dawned on him. He simply said, "may God forgive you." And I simply said, "Amen."

I did not understand this dream and my subsequent action until 1996, twenty two years ago, while I was in deep meditation. The dream came back to my mind. It was vivid. And the silent voice in my abyss of thought explained that the two men I saw standing guard at the gate of my father represent Christianity and Islam, my father represent "God" and my speaking directly with my father represents my eventual evolution as a mystic.

Few years ago, I think it was 2015 if I am not mistaken, someone said to me "I have wanted to ask Mr Fayemi this. Why does he always describe himself as a 'mystic'? From all appearance his aphorisms are more sage, wise, than mystical. Just wondering. Or the mystical side is shielded from us - the uninitiated!" And I responded: "I describe myself as a mystic, modern mystic to be precise (I use the scientific method), and not the type you read in books, but a mystic nonetheless, because the source of my writings is a silent voice in my abyss of thoughts. I call it "Something that Speaks but is not Seen" A mystic, it has been said, is fundamentally a philosopher."I don't have ANY religion though. However I have evolved into a mystic. And a mystic is fundamentally a philosopher. I do not really attach a label to myself. I simply live, love, unfold, evolve. And when the bell tolls, as it eventually must, I would love to have become the best that I could have become. Hence I must continually strive for change, for growth.

Conversation with "God"
Year 2000

"God:" "Stop praying."

Me: "Stop praying? You must not be "God" Everyone that believes in "God" prays."

So I kept on praying ceaselessly.

A year passed.

"God:" "Your prayers are not being answered."

That was true. None of my prayer in the preceding year was answered.

Hmmmm.

"God:" "You are reaping what you sowed. No amount of prayer can change that."

"God:" "While you are here, I will teach you how to live a lifestyle, one contrary to the one that brought you here, a lifestyle of striving to do the right things the right way, in all things, and at all times."

I wrestled with this for a while. I got angry. I even cursed "God" out. I told "Him" to take "His" miserable life back, that I did not want it again.

I was depressed for a period of time. Not ordinary sorrow, but the type that required taking antidepressants for.

Then the lessons of life began by the silent voice in my abyss of thoughts. And the depression lifted, the enjoyment of simple pleasures of life that I had taken for granted resumed. I went on to master "ordinary human emotions" and the thinking that produces them. That was how I acquired my emotional equilibrium. Peace came first, followed by contentment. My heart then became a fertile ground for love to bloom. You can now dance "Shoki" inside my belly, frolicking in the juice of my joy. That was eighteen years ago. That was how and when I stopped praying. That was when disappointment, frustration sadness/sorrow fled. That was when I truly began to live, love and laugh.

Look at me now. Look at me again. Don't you see how my "outrageous misfortune" became "God's" blessing in disguise?

CHAPTER 5

WHEN THE STUDENT IS READY

By December of 1993, I realized that I was on life's dead end. I knew that I had to change my illegal lifestyle, my illegal way of making money. But I did not change fast enough. The consequences of not changing fast enough became my era of trial and tribulation, which is a subject of another book. During this era of trial and tribulation, which spanned about eleven years, I began to change my ways. I vowed not to ever take part in any illegal activity. I began to retrain myself and invested my time in personal development. This was between 1994 and 1996.

In 1996, my brother, Niyi, sent me two books. One of the books was "The Prince" by Nicolo Machiavelli. The second one was "The Art of Dreaming" by Carlos Castaneda. In the book, "Art of Dreaming", I read that someone can set up his own dream. Really? That night, before I slept off, I decided to set up my own dream. I wished to dream about my children. And I truly dreamed about one of my children, Shola. In the dream, I saw Shola sitting on a fence.

She was undecided whether to be on this side of the fence or the other side. Her teeth were very dirty. She appeared unkept. Then I woke up from the dream. Okay. So it was indeed possible for someone to set up his own dream. When I woke up the next morning, I called Shola's grandmother to find out how my daughter was doing. "Hi ma," I said.

"Koolie, am glad that you called. The Department of Child Welfare is looking for Traci. They are trying to take her children away from her because, they said, she was not taking good care of the children."

Wow!

My dream was very close to reality.

The next morning I went to the Christian chaplain at the chapel near me. A "chaplain is a minister, such as a priest, pastor , rabbi, imam or lay representative of a religious tradition, attached to a secular institution such as a hospital, prison, military unit, school, police department, university, or private chapel." Wikipedia. I explained my experience to the chaplain, who incidentally happened to have a master's degree in psychology. He told me that the book I read was fiction. Okay. But how fictitious could it be if I could do as it said and it worked? When he realized I was not going to take no for an answer, he said he could bring me a book that would teach me how my dream would not come true again. This man was not getting it. Here I was, trying to learn more about my experience and this man was saying something else?

Finally, he told me he would bring a book on Christian meditation for me. And that was the first time I heard anything about meditation.

The first book the chaplain brought, "The Other Side of Silence: Meditation for the Twenty-First Century by Morton T. Kelsey", taught me how to meditate. However, it tried to guide me to focus my mind on stories from the bible. My mind, feeling like it was being programmed, rebelled. I went back to the chaplain and he brought another book for me: "The Experience of Insight" by Joseph Goldstein. I found this book insightful and liberating. It taught me two types of meditation: choice less awareness and directed awareness.

In choice less awareness, one simply sits in meditation, concentrating on one's breathing, and let whatever comes to come. But in directed awareness, one focuses on something in particular, like a vexing problem that needs to be solved, a concept in need of a deeper understanding etc.

Within one week of learning meditation, my inner life came alive. I began to see images in my meditation. And my intuition accelerated.

Sometimes after, I was in meditation and I saw a clock. The big hand of the clock ran and stopped at twelve and the small hand ran and stopped at three. Intuition said it was 3:00pm. Then I saw two police officers taking this African American guy that I usually play chess with, away in handcuffs. I came out of meditation. The time was around 11am. I went looking for the roommate of the guy I just saw being led away in handcuffs. He was from Granada. And to him, my name was Africa.

I told him what I just saw in my meditation. We then went our separate ways. Unbeknownst to Granada and me, his African American roommate had a problem with some guys out of New York and they decided to beat him up. Once he became aware of this, he quietly made a call to the police officers and requested to be taken into protective custody for his safety. It was exactly 3:00pm when he was led away, in handcuffs, to protective custody.

At another time, I lay down on my bed and covered myself from head to toe with a bed sheet. I got into meditation and shortly after, a guy named Alvin came in. He was cooking for the two of us and I knew he came to pick up my bowl. Before he spoke, I told him to pick my bowl on top of my locker. He did, and he left.

Soon after I finished my meditation and uncovered myself. That was when the new experience dawned on me: how did I know it was Alvin that came in when my eyes were closed and I had a bed sheet covering me from head to toe? This experience taught me that some people could "see" mentally. Call it spiritually if you like. Verification is still the best way to know those who could "see."

However, sometimes, instead of seeing images in my meditation, a complete sentence would come out of my silent mind. Some of these sentences are: "Half book of half truths." "Ideals are good but practicality is what always matter." "Go through the same channel" etc.

I have since made "ideals are good but practicality is what always matter" my personal motto.

During another Meditation session, a profound, liberating sense of freedom from within erupted from the depth of my being. This feeling is akin to the feeling one feels after a rope tying one down is let loose. Joyously, I began to say to myself, "I am free! I am free!"

Dark Nights of the Soul.

In the same 1996, I went through my dark nights of the soul, my "coldest winter" ever." For about a week, I could not sleep well. I was very miserable. Depression took the thrill, the joy, the sweet out of my life. Things that I had done in the past, some that I could not consciously remember, came to my mind. The consequences of those things I have done also came to my mind. They joined together like Siamese twin. It was amazing. It was like watching a movie to see its climax. I obtain my knowledge that "I always reap what I sow" from this inner experience. That was when it dawn on me that I was the one, through my thinking, my actions, and my relationship with others that manufactured my negative consequences. Upon that realization, like a fog, misery lifted, leaving in its wake my customary inner joy and peace. That was when I vowed to always strive to do the right things, the right way, at all times, in all things.

CHAPTER 6

ACCELERATION OF INTUITION

Intuition is the ability to understand something immediately without the need for conscious reasoning. Intuition aids human enlightenment by giving insight into certain concepts that were previously unknown.

Anyone can be intuitive, regardless of whether they are religious or not, regardless of whether they believe in "God" or not. In my own world, the results produced, and not the story told, are the evidence of accelerated intuition. Meditation is known to enhance intuition.

What Is Meditation? Meditation is simply a breathing exercise with a focus on in and out breathing. Just like going to the gym helps to develop the muscles, Meditation helps to develop sharpness of the mind. It is for those who want to develop their minds, their innate human resources. It is to clean, calm your mind and immersed it in better, pertinent knowledge. There is a part of our brain that meditation awakens. And that part provides guidance in doing the right things, the right way, in all things, and at all times.

I use meditation to train my mental muscles. And it has awakened me beyond my conditioned mind and habitual thinking. When my mind is calm and silent, yet completely alert, I always experience a state of profound, deep peace. Like I wrote earlier, I learned two types of meditation in 1996: choice less awareness and directed awareness. In choice less awareness, one simply sit in meditation, concentrating on one's in and out breathing, and letting whatever comes to come. But in directed awareness, one focuses on something in particular, like a vexing problem that needs to be solved, a concept in need of a deeper understanding etc.

Within one week of learning meditation, my inner life came alive. I began to see images in my meditation. And my intuition accelerated. This was the first image I saw in my meditation. I saw a giant standing. Then he bent down, slowly to pick up an adult human that appeared like a baby in comparison to the giant. He held the human to his chest. And he was caressing the back of the human. Think of a loving father holding his one day old baby to his chest. That was the exact image I saw. Intuition told me this was the Giant of Love. There were small one-day-old-looking, but adult humans all around. There was a pit. And there was a long line of humans inside this pit. Again, intuition told me this was the Pit of Misery.

I saw myself, in Superman outfit, flying all around the Giant of Love. I would carry the small humans, one at a time, to the giant. And the giant would give him/her the loving caress of a doting father. Then, natural knowing allowed me to know that my next assignment was to go deep inside the Pit of Misery and bring out one small human. This small human would then be transformed into a Superman, like me, doing what I was doing also. Instead of me to be happy that I would have someone to be assisting me and the giant, I recoiled at the idea. The word "Jealousy" began to flash in mind. Jealousy! Imagine that. I had never seen myself as a jealous person. But jealousy was buried down inside the core of my being. It was just waiting for the right time to rear its head in my life. I instantly knew that jealousy was one of the negative emotions I had to get rid of in order to continue to grow in my meditation.

There are many different ways to practice meditation. The method I used most of the time is done this way: I lie down on my bed. Sometimes, I cover my body with bed sheet to avoid distractions. Sometimes I do not. I relax all my muscles. I remove my awareness from my surrounding. I concentrate on my in and out breathing by counting from one to hundred. I lie there until my body begins to feel as if I am sleeping. However, my mind is always alive underneath. This, I call "Trance state." I just stay there and wait for whatever might happen.

Sometimes I see images without understanding what they mean. Sometimes I understand what the images mean. Sometimes I let ideas, thoughts, and images roam freely through my mind with the hope that they may lead to some new solutions to certain vexing problems. Sometimes I just lie there and enjoy the peace and calmness that come from within. Sometimes I experience a state of mystical awareness of "God's" being. Sometimes I learn more about myself. Sometimes I see familiar things in a different way. Sometimes I acquire new knowledge. Sometimes I catch a glimpse of the past and the future. Sometimes the understanding of my dreams comes to me. All the time I hear the voice now. But the voice was absent in the beginning. Sometimes I try not to think of anything and just blank out my mind with no conscious awareness.

Meditation, like I have said, is a breathing exercise. It is to the mind what the gym is to the body. Those who spend quality time cultivating their mind will get fulfilling moments harvesting its output. What can a human do without his/her mind? Is the mind not the tool used in perceiving, believing, deciding? A malfunctioning mind will ruin the life of its possessor. And a beautiful mind will not only produce success and happiness for its possessor, it will also produce contentment. You are still wondering why you should master meditation? I recommend that you learn and practice meditation.

The same year I learned meditation, 1996, I was in deep meditation, praying--yes, praying. I used to pray then--for knowledge, wisdom, and understanding. After the customary calmness and stillness of mind that meditation induces, I silently "heard"--or was it "know"?--"Go through the same channel." Go through the same channel how? I thought I could pray and get knowledge, wisdom, and understanding from a dream. I thought wrong.

Again, in 1997, I was in meditation. And I felt that I was going deeper than before. Then, I suddenly began to feel a sense of apprehension that bordered on fear. Why should I be afraid to go deeper into myself? Intuition spoke silently again: "go and learn what is known and come back for what's unknown."

Okay. That was when my appetite for knowledge got bigger and my thirst for knowledge increased. I began to spend most of my waking time in the library, soaking in what was known in preparation to go back inward for what was unknown. These were the things that I had to acquire through conscious, continuous striving. By 1997, a silent voice surfaced in my meditation and took over the teaching that is still going on up until today.

One of the objectives of meditation is to stop thinking, to go beyond thinking and rely on intuition. It may take longer than you think to achieve result in your meditation. Sometimes it does. But you must resist taking short cuts. With patience, constant practice, you will ultimately achieve excellent results.

A lot of people have not been taught how to think. They have been taught what to think. And they simply recall those information and they think they are thinking. Meditation will help you to clear the debris of your mind by melting what others have taught you to think, to believe, and you will begin to think, creatively, innovatively, positively, for yourself.

One of the goals of meditation is to develop power of the mind. Those who have power of the mind can manifest that power by the productions of their minds. Effective living, cell phones, good systems, airplanes, ships, televisions are few examples of productions of the mind. And those with weakness of the mind can also manifest that weakness by the production of their minds. Ineffective living, stories of past performances and old glories, more stories of unprovable subjects, delusion are few example of weakness of the mind. I have move beyond stories, to the development the power of mind. I am tired of telling "proveless" stories.

Drones are weapons of war, a manifestation of the technological advancement of some human beings. The operator of the drone merely sits in an air-conditioned room, far away from harm's way, sipping coffee, smoking a cigarette, using joystick to remote control unmanned plane that targets and bombs suspected terrorists/enemies. And what do some other people have as manifestations of their "untechnological advancement"? Some people sending "holy ghost fire" to kill their enemies. Some people tag natural, preventable, treatable ailments as "spiritual attacks" from the enemy. Still others get bombed and do nothing, believing that their self defense is not in their hands but in "God's" hands. To bridge this technological gap, our minds must evolve creatively. Or else... Others will continue to make aircrafts while those who refused to evolve will continue to make witchcrafts. Both are some form of craft. Not so?

Everyone has muscles. But not everyone is "cut up". Those with finely chiseled body, bulging biceps, flat tummy, have invested time in the gym, on the tracks, to arrive at that destination. They eat balanced diet that complement their rigorous workouts. It is neither by juju/charm, nor by prayer. They simply followed a disciplined workout regimen. They nurtured what nature had provided for them. The same analogy can be applied to the human mind. Everyone has a mind. Not so? I am now assuming that the mind houses the human intelligence. Therefore, the mind is akin to the control center, the determinant factor for the effective utilization of all the other human resources/talents. Without a sound mind, no matter how strong the body is, the chance of becoming a load carrier at Oyingbo Market increases, the chance of being poor, high. The mind is the tool for acquiring knowledge, wisdom, and understanding. And these come through focused, disciplined study. They come from observation, experimentation, and verification. They also come from experience, intuition, and creative thinking. Did you hear me mention juju/ charm/praying? Ok, you did not. That is because leading countries of the world use the former formula and not the latter. And anyone that is interested in excellence, in leading, in living a fulfilling life devoid of problems, must learn how to do the right things the right way, in all things, and at all times. Nature/Providence/God has provided the raw materials. Failure to develop, refine those raw materials is the essence of stagnation, subjugation.

Like I said, Nature/God has already provided all the materials (input) we need to be successful, to be happy, and to continually add value to our society. However, we need to master the ways and means (process) to turn these provided materials into desirable, favorable lives/ products (output). Potential is not actual. But potential can be transformed to actual with the mastery of the input-process-output model.

Truth and delusion, unfortunately, spring from the same Source. It is through verification and experience we can separate one from the other. We must be cautious when we think abstractly. We must protect our mental health by installing verifying "devices" inside our head. I know this because my mind used to lie to me a lot. It still does, but less and less. It would manufacture opinions that were wrong. It would make me believe things that were not truthful. And it would deceive me and made me accept other people's assumptions, superstitions, without verification. But when I learned how to meditate, just the breathing exercise, it cleared my mind of most of its debris. It melted away most of my erroneous opinions, assumptions, and superstitions. It allowed me to know that I did not know as much as I thought I knew. It birthed my curiosity, ignited my passion to learn, to know. Consequently, it transported me to the psychological territory where intuition accelerated. That was when I discovered the importance of doing the right things the right way, in all things, and at all times. And creativity, the replacing of old lifestyle with a new and better, more satisfying, more fulfilling one ensued. And happiness gushed, love bloomed.

Do you have a need for self-respect, strength, competence, mastery, self-confidence, independence, and freedom? Then meditation is for you. You can use meditation to develop the inner competence derived from experience. Practicing meditation requires no change in belief or lifestyle.

No matter what station you are, if as at today, you do not feel fulfilled, if you are mostly unhappy, you are doing some things wrong. Happiness is a by-product of fulfilling activities. And everyone, I repeat, everyone has the human ability to be happy. It is those simple choices we routinely make that are responsible for either our happiness or our pain. I see people, a lot of people, struggling to put a 20kg load on a stand designed to carry a 10kg load. Of course they are not stupid people. They are only trying to follow the dictates of their religion, of their culture. As for me, I neither struggle, nor suffer. I simply put a 10kg load on a stand designed to carry a 10kg load. As a mystical creative rebel, I stay afloat, even in troubling times. I live, love, laugh, without religious, cultural encumbrance.

CHAPTER 7

THE ADVENT OF THE VOICE

When the voice first surfaced in my meditation, I was not so sure if it was my own thinking or not. But as time went on, I was convinced that it was different from my thinking. The voice said he is "God."

While consuming all the spiritual books I could lay my hands on, I had read in one book that eventually a voice would surface in my meditation. But I was instructed to banish the voice and continue with my meditation. So, naturally, when the voice surfaced, I wanted it banished. But how? When I could not do it on my own, I sought the assistance of a psychiatrist who prescribed a psychotropic drug for me. The drug worked, or so it seemed. I would not hear what the voice was saying, but I would simply know via intuition. Up until today, I neither know how to banish the voice, nor do I want to.

CONVERSATION WITH "GOD"

"God:" "Even though you were raised as a Christian, you are very ignorant of the other world's religions. Go back and study all those religions. Aro meta ki nda obe nu. At least study the three major ones in your country."

Me: The three major ones? But I know of only Christianity and Islam.

God: Chuckling, "Don't you know Ifa is part of the traditional African religion?"

Me: "Of course I do not know."

God: "Ifa is the oracular deity in the original Yoruba religion. And your lineage used to be Ifa priests but abandoned it for Christianity"

Me: But why study all religions when I am not even religious?"

God: "You have to learn what is known already. Then come back later to learn what is unknown."

Hmmmmmm.

I found out that the world has over 4000 religions!

So, I studied all the World's major religions, about ten in number, but refused to study the Ifa religion. Who wanted to go back to archaic religion? Not me.

Growing up, I had been inculcated with the belief that those practicing the traditional African religions were idol worshipers, that they worship Satan. The more I thought about this childhood conditioning, the more my resolution not to study the Ifa religion.

Then depression descended; clinical depression, not mere sadness and sorrow. Life lost its pleasant allurement.
Naturally, I sought the psychologist's assistance. This was in Allenwood, Pennsylvania.

After several hours of counseling, the American psychologist, who was white and a Christian, advised me to honor the unseen voice's instruction. He gave me a clean bill of psychological health by saying there was nothing wrong with me apart from cognitive dissonance. He said my Subjective Reality ought to be in Alignment with my Objective Reality.

Okay. So I studied the Ifa religion. And I found it not to be compatible with my evolved mind.

Thereafter, like a fog, the depression lifted, leaving inner peace and inner joy in its place.
But...

I learned two vital concepts from my study of Ifa:

The first one is, eni ti o ba se otito ju ni Ifa ma ngbe. Ifa favours the most honest.

The second one is that the Ifa priest, as a prerequisite to making any sacrifice, must offer a sacrifice to Esu. This stems from the belief that Olodumare (God) has empowered Esu to cause disturbance anywhere good things are been done. So, to prevent Esu from coming to disturb his good sacrifice, the priest "give unto Ceaser what is Ceaser's".

Of course this sounds logical to me as a concept, even if not as a practice.

And I have since incorporated that concept into my thinking and implanted it into my behavior.

I have since "sacrificed" all the thinking and behavior that prevented the doing the right things the right way, if not in all things, in most things, if not at all times, most of the time.

This, to me, is true salvation.

CONVERSATION WITH "GOD"
YEAR 2000

"God:" "Stop praying."

Me: "Sop praying? You must not be "God" Everyone that believes in God prays."

So I kept on praying ceaselessly.

A year passed.

"God:" "Your prayers are not being answered."

That was true. None of my prayer in the preceding year was answered.

Hmmmm.

"God:" "You are reaping what you sowed. No amount of prayer can change that."

"God:" "While you are here, I will teach you how to live a lifestyle, one contrary to the one that brought you here, a lifestyle of striving to do the right things the right way, in all things, and at all times."

I wrestled with this for a while. I got angry. I even cursed "God" out. I told "Him" to take "His" miserable life back, that I did not want it again.

I was depressed for a period of time. Not ordinary sorrow, but the type that required taking antidepressants for.

Then the lessons of life began by the silent voice in my abyss of thoughts. And the depression lifted, the enjoyment of simple pleasures of life that I had taken for granted resumed. I went on to master "ordinary human emotions" and the thinking that produces them. That was how I acquired my emotional equilibrium. Peace came first, followed by contentment. My heart then became a fertile ground for love to bloom. You can now dance "Shoki" inside my belly, frolicking in the juice of my joy. That was seventeen years ago. That was how and when I stopped praying. That was when disappointment, frustration sadness/sorrow fled. That was when I truly began to live, love and laugh.

Look at me now. Look at me again. Don't you see how my "outrageous misfortune" became "God's" blessing in disguise?

CONVERSATION WITH "GOD"
YEAR 2000.

"God:" You are afraid to live in Nigeria because you do not want to suffer."

Me: "Yes. After all these years in the US, I cannot cope with that suffering and smiling of no light, no water, no good roads etc."

"God:" "With your vow that you will no longer get involved in corrupt practices, I can guarantee you that you will not suffer in Nigeria. That is where your purpose of life is. That is where you will a life that has meaning."

This is 2018. My pact with "God" in 2000 is still going strong. The sun does not "smite me during the day or the moon by night." Ideals are good. But practicality is what always matter. And obligations and entitlement are irrevocably linked.

I have always maintained that prayer is an exercise in futility if not coupled with "doing the right things the right way, in all things, and at all times." Having effective religious, political, and traditional leaders who inspire, compel us to do the right things, the right way, in all things, and at all times is the solution to most countries' problems. No one can plant corn and reap beans. No amount of praying and fasting can achieve that.

CHAPTER 8
MY ENCOUNTER WITH DELUSION

In 1996, I woke up one day and simply believed that I would be able to speak Spanish if I earnestly prayed to "God", even though I had not learned Spanish. After all, nothing is impossible for "God". I did pray earnestly. And I did believe that I would be able to speak and understand Spanish afterwards. So, I told a Mexican guy to speak Spanish to me. But I could not understand one single thing he was saying. And I could not speak a single word of Spanish. It was after that I developed my motto that "ideals are good but practicality is what always matter."

Beware of delusion. Beware of false beliefs. It wastes time. And it takes focus and effort away from what is real, what is practicable. And it produces failure on the long run. Delusion lurks in the human mind. And verification can mitigate it. If you believe you can do something but have not done it yet, if you believe you have something but no one can verify it, come to me and take a delusion test. I will show you the faint but certain trace of delusion lurking in that mind. And I will prescribe a cure for you. Delusion is the chief culprit in every disappointment, in every false expectation, in every unrealistic hope. Be aware.

WHAT IS FAITH?

"Faith is to believe what you do not see; the reward of this faith is to see what you believe.' St. Augustine.

Who is St. Augustine? According to Wikipedia, "Augustine of Hippo was an early Christian theologian and philosopher whose writings influenced the development of Western Christianity and Western philosophy. He was the bishop of Hippo Regius, located in Numidia."

I find his quote on faith very relevant to my experience. I have since discovered that a very thin line separates faith from delusion. Faith, of course, always works, always. But delusion never works, never. A deluded person is always in a perpetual waiting mode for illusory promises. And I have seen people that have elevated delusion to the level of faith.

Faith is essentially to trust that something will happen and it does. Faith has truth as its foundation. Delusion is to trust that something will happen and it does not. It has lies as its foundation. There is a clear difference. The more one believes in something that is not true, the more stagnant one is going to become. It is as simple as ABC.

Definition of Delusion: expecting, hoping, and praying for things that will never happen. Doing things the wrong way, yet expecting the right results is delusional. False beliefs that will never manifest in concrete reality are delusion. Unrealistic expectations are the children of delusion. Delusion is dangerous. It impedes progress by directing efforts towards retrogressive projects. If you have been expending efforts, but without commensurate progress, take a test for detection of delusion. Delusion can be mild or acute. I need to take a test for detection of delusion. Is mine mild or acute? I have been expending efforts for ten years, to bring about desirable change, but without commensurate progress. Is it not delusional to expect change from people that are unwilling or unable to change?

Faith without work is said to be dead. Prayer is an act of faith. It is not work. Beliefs are elements of faith. They are not work. Tithing, seedings, night vigils, pilgrimage to Mecca and Jerusalem etc are religious rituals. They are not work. What, then, is this work that is so fundamental to making faith come alive? In modern language, it is the input-process-output model. This is the foundation of all things produced by humans. Those who have mastered, and continually implement the input-process-output model, succeed. Those who ignore it, fail.

What is input-process-output model?

Let us say you want to always have food in your house. Becoming a farmer will be one good option. Acquiring lands, farm helps, seedlings etc are quintessential. They are your inputs. The actual cultivation of the land, weeding and watering, etc these are your processes.

Aha!

The harvest, the real reason behind your striving that is your output. Failing to go through the required necessary steps and praying ceaselessly is an exercise in futility. It is a clear sign of someone who does not love the truth. And the reward for not loving the truth is: "And for this cause God shall send them strong delusion, that they should believe a lie: That they all might be damned who believed not the truth, but had pleasure in unrighteousness."

Ladies and gentlemen, stop your self-delusion. There is no substitute for doing the right things the right way. Stop chasing shadows. No one is known to ever catch one.

Creative, innovative thinking, meditation, researching, verification are some of the processes, the work required to bring good things to life!
Regardless of all our religious observance, if we do not have the love of truth, "God" will send us a strong dosage of delusion, and we will believe lies. Believing lies and acting on them waste time, efforts, with no favorable results. In addition, because the mind does not have the capacity to know what is true or not, it is the responsibility of lovers of truth to test all things to ascertain their veracity before stamping anything as true. The truth always works. If most things are working well in our life, that is good for us. That is the clearest sign that we have mitigated delusion

The reason we put so much effort, so much commitment into any endeavor is to achieve desirable and favorable result, within reasonable time frame. If the effort, the commitment is coupled with the right and truthful knowledge, thinking/beliefs, it will yield the desired, favorable result. But if the effort, the commitment is coupled with half truths, lies, and delusions, the desired, favorable result will never come, leading to frustration, anger, and disappointment. Get rid of delusion, and half-truths, outright lies will disappear, taking frustration, anger and disappointment with them.

CHAPTER 9
CLARITY

Thinking is the essence of everything created by humans. Thinking can be classified as useful or useless, valuable or valueless, creative or destructive, old or new, ethical or unethical. Thinking that is new and useful, that is creative and valuable, and that is ethical and legal ultimately create new values for the individual, for the society. A continually new-values-creating society is a less corrupt one.

Take a mental audit today: Is your thinking creating new values for yourself and your society? Can you or anyone honestly say his/her life has gotten better because of your thinking? The gate of change is within each individual. And only that individual can fling that door open. So if any segment of your thinking is the opposite of those mentioned above, it is time to commence the change process. We must create the type of society that we, and our lineage, can live in comfortably, and be proud of ultimately.

"Happiness will come to you when it comes from you. Success will be yours when you choose to take responsibility for making it so." One of the requirements of success and happiness is the ability to think accurately. One that does not think accurately cannot make effective decisions. And effective decisions are the foundation of lasting success and enduring happiness. Meditation will enable you to see old familiar things in a new, better way, thereby giving you more opportunities to make better decisions, to solve problems effectively. "Meditation brings many benefits: It refreshes us, helps us settle into what's happening now, makes us wiser and gentler, helps us cope in a world that overloads us with information and communication, and it makes us more productive."

"Problem-solving and decision-making are closely linked, and each requires creativity in identifying and developing options." Intuition and creativity are closely linked. Meditation can improve the quality of your intuition, and consequently, your creativity. Intuition aids human enlightenment by giving insight into certain concepts that were previously unknown. Anyone can be intuitive. Meditation enhances intuition. Meditation will keep you balanced, keep you focused on doing the things that will lead to enduring happiness and lasting success.

The cause of a lot of problems is ignorance rooted in delusion. That type of ignorance is very resistant to reasoning. Therefore it is impervious. It is very injurious to the self and a dangerous menace to society. Its weight keeps a society down, frolicking in stagnation. And the cure is......."We cannot solve a problem with the same level of thinking that created them." Acquire acuity. Refine your thoughts. Elevate it to its useful potential where it can serve you well. That is why we have functional brains. Stop stopping where they stopped. Growth, progress is not achieved that way. Go beyond what is known, into the territory of the unknown. That is how to bring new things to life. That is how to become leaders of thoughts.

Frustration is defined as "a feeling of dissatisfaction, often accompanied by anxiety or depression, resulting from unfulfilled needs or unresolved problem" Do you a favor by pinpointing the areas of these unresolved problems and unfulfilled needs and consider making changes that will afford you the peace you desire and so desperately need. Life is too short to live it in a state of aggravation. Free yourself from these chains that have limited and even stopped your forward progress and inner peace. Be brave, confront these facts, address them one by one and make the necessary adjustments to live your life the way you truly desire.
I truly think life is complex, not easy. But the complexity of life can be simplified by our intelligence, our thinking, our behavior. Adequate knowledge and superb foresight are some of the quintessential for making effective life-simplifying decisions that prevent, solve vexing problems. You want a stress-free, satisfying

life? Then you must master objective reality, not only as it ought to be, but also as it is. Only then can you simplify and not complicate it.

"Ti a ba de oju, a ri imu." If we squint in the direction of our nose, we will be able to see our nose. Life does not do as it like, meaning it is not capricious. Behind the apparent worldly chaos, there is order. There are natural laws that govern the universe. That knowledge is accessible to those who strive to access it. Life is art and science combined. The science part is the fixed laws. The art part is what you do, creatively or otherwise, with the fixed part. Nature has provided. But we must nurture. Nature is unkind to those who fail to nurture. And, failure to nurture always leads to underdevelopment, to stagnation, then, to retrogression. Make nurturing all your "hidden Human Resources" a priority henceforth. To believe is on a lower level than to know. And ignorance is on a higher level than delusion. In addition, it is only a thin line that separates stability from stagnation. It is innovation that can ensure that stability does not degenerate into stagnation.

Power, in all its meanings, is simply the ability to achieve. Possession of power makes most goals and objective achievable. To be without it is to sit back and wait until it is acquired. It may be delusional for one to brag about possessing power, and yet be unable to utilize it skillfully. Power of the mind precedes the manifestation of it externally. Develop it. Everyone has muscle. But not everyone is "cut up". Those with finely chiseled body, bulging biceps, flat tummy have invested time in the gym, on the tracks, to arrive at that destination. They eat balanced diet that complement their rigors workouts. It is neither by juju/charm, nor by prayer. They simply followed a disciplined workout regimen. They nurtured what nature had provided for them. The same analogy can be applied to the human mind. Everyone has a mind. Not so? I am now assuming that the mind houses the human intelligence. Therefore, the mind is akin to the control center, the determinant factor for the effective utilization of all the other human resources/talents. Without a sound mind, no matter how strong the body is the chance of becoming a load carrier at Oyingbo Market increases, the chance of being poor, high. The mind is the tool for acquiring knowledge, wisdom, and understanding. And these come through focused, disciplined study, observation, experimentation, verification, experience, intuition, creative thinking. Did you hear me mention juju/charm/praying? Ok, you did not. That is because leading countries of the world use the former formula and not the latter. And anyone interested in excellence, in leading, in living a fulfilling life devoid of problems, must learn how to do the right things the right way, in all things, and at all times.

Our thinking/beliefs can either help or harm us. If our thinking/belief is true, it can guide us, protect our emotions, and preserve our relationships.

But if it is wrong, it can misguide us, harm our emotions, disturbs our relationships. The chief culprit in the generation of negative feelings is erroneous thinking/belief. Verifying the veracity of our thinking/belief is, therefore, an antidote to negative emotions. Truth always lessens disappointment. What one expects does not disappoint. For example:

If I already think/believe that it will rain later today, then I will not plan anything rain can disturb. And if it does rain, I will not be disappointed. As a matter of fact, I will be elated. However, if it does not rain as thought, or as believed, then I may be disappointed. And the intensity of that disappointment may affect my emotions, my relationships. So, anyone that wants to cleanse his/her negative emotions ought to verify the veracity of our thinking/belief in order to lesson disappointment.

We may never always get all we want, but at least we ought not to be disappointed over the things we do not get. Life can be sweet if we make it so. I have chosen to make it so. And my sweet emotions are no longer subject to the ups and downs of life.

Quality of thought is essentially the quality of truth in that thought. And quality of life is essentially quality of thought, which is essentially quality of truth in that thought. That is on the assumption that appropriate action is taking to manifest the truth in that thoughts. Because your beliefs end up to be your thoughts, always test them to ascertain their truthfulness. Strong, creative, ethical minds create strong, creative, ethical systems, institutions, society. Weak, primitive, unethical minds create weak, stagnating, unethical systems, institutions, society. "It is not wisdom if we simply believe what we are told. True wisdom is to directly see and understand for ourselves. At this level then, wisdom is to keep an open mind rather than being closed-minded, listening to other points of view rather than being bigoted; to carefully examine facts that contradict our beliefs, rather than burying our heads in the sand; to be objective rather than prejudiced and partisan; to take time about forming our opinions and beliefs rather than just accepting the first or most emotional thing that is offered to us; and to always be ready to change our beliefs when facts that contradict them are presented to us. A person who does this is certainly wise and is certain to eventually arrive at true understanding." ~Ven. S. Dhammika

"The happiness of your life depends upon the quality of your thoughts." Enhance the quality of your thoughts through meditation. Do not be like those dangerous people that have made some mistakes, that are making some mistakes, yet they are not aware that they have made the mistakes, that they are making some mistakes. Instead, they will blame others, witches and wizards for their misfortunes, which are consequences of their mistakes. Some mistakes are truly consequences of erroneous thinking, bad choices, and ineffective decisions. With meditation, you can observe your thoughts as they are rising in your mind. With critical thinking skills, you can analyze the consequences of your actions before you act. A well-knitted lifestyle must be planned and not just hoped for. Proper planning is known to prevent poor performance.

Beliefs are basic. Practice is paramount. And for me, ideals are good. But practicality is what always matter. Faith that is not coupled with sound reasoning/logic will wither into superstition. Imagine a man that wants bulging muscles. He reads a book on how to develop muscles. He believes going to work out at the gym will work wonders. But he stops there. And he brags about his knowledge of muscle building. On the long run, a Mile 12 Market load carrier will have more muscles than him. If you don't believe me, just come to Nigeria and see plenty of evidence to back up my assertion. With a lot of people, superstitions have supplanted sound reasoning. And the obvious manifestation of this is lack of growth, of progress in their lives. Sound reasoning, strong logic, verification, are essentials for spiritual/psychological development. Without them, delusion, which is simply false belief, will reign freely in the minds of the uncritical thinkers. Creativity is finding new ways of doing something in a better way. So, what type of creativity can be expected from those who are fond of thinking the same thoughts, saying the same things, doing the same things, the same way, years after years?

With the totality of our thinking/beliefs in consideration, are we stagnant, growing, or regressing? This is a question we all ought to ask ourselves. Growth and stability must be constant in our lives. Using outdated thoughts/beliefs is not compatible with growth. It is not compatible with stability. Let us ask our phone of ten years ago. We simply have to start thinking creatively, innovatively, and critically, if we want to call ourselves thinkers. We have to know the current state of truth. By the way, the scientific method, a modern method of inquiry, starts with an observation, experience, thoughts. Then, hypothesis is formulated. And, facts are gathered to prove or disprove the hypothesis. If the facts prove the veracity of the hypothesis, it is called truth. But if the facts disprove the hypothesis, then, the hypothesis is declared untrue. Therefore, making unverified statement to contradict a known fact is the hallmark of a lazy, shabby thinker, definitely not compatible with growth, progress, stability.

CHAPTER 10
MODERN SPIRITUALITY

Spirituality simply means to go beyond the known, the seen, into the unknown, unseen. Vision is one of the derivatives of spirituality. And, it is common knowledge that vision and leadership are the two sides of the same coin.

Spirituality is the "inside-out" approach. You simply allow what is within you to unfold, without prejudice, with critical thinking, with constant verification. That, in my opinion, is the real "spiritual" growth. Is it not written that the kingdom of "God" is within you?

The core of any religion is spirituality. But, a lot of religionists are not into spirituality. Or to put it another way, spirituality, which is to transcend the physical, is not into them. Accurate vision is the clearest manifestation of true spirituality. A lot of religious houses have become the mansions of delusion, where strong delusion reigns as king. Is it not written that "God" Himself will send strong delusion to those who do not love the truth so that they can believe lies? How can anyone who does not prove, test, and verify all things claim to love the truth?

What a lot of people called interpretation is truly a distortion of the truth. True interpretation ought to fit our shared reality. Accurate Interpretation of reality brings contentment. Distortion of reality ultimately brings dissatisfaction. In the abundance of "water" some people are thirsty.

Largely, spiritual guidance is not inside books. It seeps directly into the human mind. And It is not speaking in tongues. "Glossolalia or speaking in tongues, according to linguists, is the fluid vocalizing of speech-like syllables that lack any readily comprehended meaning, in some cases as part of religious practice in which it is believed to be a divine language unknown to the speaker." Those who know, know.

The truly guided, whether secular or spiritual, live an orderly life and not one in disarray. They live a contented life and not one of perpetual lacking, not one of unending dissatisfaction.

Repeating what happened over two thousand years ago, or merely repeating what has been written at any time is not what spirituality is about. Spiritual growth is quite different from religiosity. It is deeper, and it manifests in one's thinking and behavior. "Spiritual growth means advancing in all forms of conversation through deep understanding of knowledge which is devoid of delusion." You can call it mental or psychological growth. Different names, same manifestation. And spiritual growth is not about repeating ancient stories. It is about living a fulfilling life. It is about enjoying the "fruits of the spirit." Mental/spiritual/psychological growth cannot be forced. It must naturally evolve. And without it, stagnation is natural.

Religious rituals, religious platitudes, do not produce the "fruits of the spirit." Upright living is still the most effective producer of verifiable "fruits". "(T)he fruit of the Spirit is love, joy, peace, forbearance, kindness, goodness, faithfulness,"

It is possible to have a "tree" without "fruits." But it is not possible to have "fruits" without a "tree." So, shouldn't a prudent person use the "fruits" to identify a fertile "tree?" That is what I do. Show me the "fruits" and I will tell you how fertile the "tree" is. Remember a fruitless tree was cursed before. Right?

According to Shakespeare, a rose flower, called by any name, will still smell the same way. And "original," called by any name, will still produce the "fruits" of the "original". Think of Ragolis, Swan, Eva etc. They are all brand names selling water. However, water is water, whether in a cup, bowl, or bottle.

Let us open our hands, not our mouth, and look into our lives. Are we truly holding the "original?" Show me the "fruits of the spirit", the blessing by "God" of the works of your hands. In your life, show me Love, joy, peace, gentleness, goodness, uprightness. Show me patience minus long-suffering, minus corruption. Show me, with your actions, the loving of your neighbors as yourself. And, if what you are holding is a fake, and therefore nothing to write home about, then, it is time to unlearn, relearn, and start afresh.

That is a tough one, is it not?

In my own book, perpetual hopes cannot replace the actual blessings of holding the "original" in our hands. The lasting pleasant sweetness that comes from the "original" is a reward for possessing it. Who feels it knows it.

If you are a mere believer, or nonbeliever, please do not pass by and just keep going about your business without reading this page. It is definitely for you too even though some things are simply not for everybody. And, if you are a knower, that is the more reason you can read on, if you will, and time permits. As a knower, you have the wherewithal to understand this page.

Anyone that claims Jesus Christ is "God" is not spiritually awakened. I repeat, anyone that claims that Jesus Christ is God is not spiritually awakened. Jesus himself said "Believest thou not that I am in the Father, and the Father in me? The words that I speak unto you I speak not of myself: but the Father that dwelleth in me, he doeth the works."

When one is spiritually awakened, he//she will know that there is a stage of spiritual growth that is called "union with God." During this stage of spiritual development, the Spirit of God dwells in the person that has gone through the discipline of becoming awakened and becoming enlightened. The spirit does not possess him/her. Instead, he/she possesses the spirit, and consequently lives uprightly, conscious of the presence of "God" in all utterances and deeds. He/she will effortlessly do the right things the right way, if not in all things, in most things, if not at all times, most of the time. No matter how lofty a spiritual stage that is, it is wrong to confuse "the man pointing to the moon for the moon." Sitting a man on the throne of "God" is not spirituality. It is definitely not spiritual knowledge. It is religion, definitely religious doctrine.

As long as we are not well versed in the art of verification, delusion will always be our ally, and propagandists, demagogues, will always be our leaders, both politically and religiously. A demagogue is "a political leader who seeks support by appealing to popular desires and prejudices rather than by using rational argument."

It continues to baffle me when some people try to remove the intellect from spirituality. It is not supposed to be so. Yes, the intellect is inadequate to access spirituality, but it is required to understand it. Anyone trying to remove intelligence, the human faculty necessary for learning and understanding, and sometimes for dealing with new and trying situation, is peddling delusion. And with delusion, the waiting period for manifestation is endless.

The foundational thoughts/beliefs in the head of most people I know are fixed, not amenable to change, not to talk of creating new ones. We are stuck for now. And stagnation is the natural consequences.

But it does not have to be this way only if we can begin to think creatively, innovatively. It is erroneous to think that condition must be right to think right. Contrarily, it is the condition that is not right that motivates one to think about what to do to make things right. After all, necessity is said to be mother of invention. And adani loro, agbara lo fi ko ni. It is during adversity that certain strengths can be developed.

It may be delusional to make decisions without having corresponding power/resources to carry out the decisions. When our desires exceed our power/resources, our mind becomes susceptible to all sorts of negativity, delusion included. We leave ourselves open to manipulation by others offering perpetual promise of everlasting solution. Promises that are perpetual: just Promises.

As an initial matter, we ought to shrink our desires to the limit of our power/resources. Then we try find creative ways to grow within the scope of our limitations. Simply put, we must cut coat according to your fabrics.

In spirituality the madman and the genius reside on the same island. However there is a thin line separating the two. While a madman "seeing" motivates him to act, his actions leads to futility. The genius' "seeing" however motivates him to act in accordance with correct principles leading to the manifestation of the gifts of spirituality. The scientific method can be used to guarantee that one does not cross that thin line into insanity (Delusion.). This is my experience. This is my type of spirituality

There is true spirituality which leads to enlightenment. An enlightened human knows right from wrong.. Her/his actions are guided by conscience. He/she strives to continually treat others with a sense of fairness. And of course she/he abstains from all forms of evil. In addition, there is junk spirituality which stems from Delusion. Anyone that is practicing junk spirituality: "his/her toil will show no profit." That is according to one of our books. In conclusion, we can "tell the tree by the fruits it bears."

Now, please analyze the following story and determine it is junk or true spirituality. Judge if it is true guidance or the delusional one.

Sometimes in 2012, my phone rang early in the morning and I picked it up, even though I mostly do not pick up unknown number calls. It was from one of my cousins that I have not since 1977. The phone connection cut as soon as she identified herself and I called her back. She said she missed my dad, her uncle, and went to visit him. She said she had a spiritual message for me, that I should come over. But because I was not interested in her spiritual message, I told her that I was not in Lagos. I told her to tell me her message on the phone. She said that I had a close friend, that I should not trust him, that if something is X, I should tell him it is Y. She said there was a family member on my mother side that was evil, that was out to revenge something done to her, that was now bent on taking revenge on me and my brother, that I should come for her to pray for me because she had the holy spirit in her. I told her that she was stupidly illogical, that by me telling my friend something was Y when it was X was in violation of my new policy of "let your yes be yes and your no be no", that by seeing any of my family as evil when there was no concrete proof, was to be malicious and evil myself. She splashed some more religious platitudes but I simply hung up the phone. Enough of wasting my valuable time in listening to complete nonsense and wasting my scare resources I used to call her back. In my opinion, I had labeled her behavior as exploitative, a clear manifestation of junk spirituality, unworthy for the truth seekers, and the preference of the delusional. My decision to be sincere and honest, not only to my friends, but also to all my associates, is irrevocable. I will rather label those who betray my trust as traitors than for them to label me as dishonest.

When I came back to Nigeria in 2005, almost everyone advised me to seek some kind of spiritual protection and guidance from the source of their choices. That was "what everyone does here", they said. I had been away from Nigeria for a long time. Could they be right? Hmmmmm! Even though I did not have any belief system, and I still do not, I decided to "test" the effectiveness of these so called spiritual guidance/protection centers.

My first test was to find out if these spiritual people could "see". And, the first two "prophets" could not "see". One, on a fishing expedition, asked me where my mother was. I answered him that my mother was in Ojodu. He said I should go and tell my mother to pray for me. If he could truly "see", he would had known that my mother was dead and was buried at Ojodu. The alfa and the babalawo I visited were just as "blind" as the first two "prophets". I could "see" clearer than all of them. So, logically, I now "see" for myself.

Even though a lot people may not see it as such. But the above is really about deficient cultural and religious leadership in some part of the world. Mental is the same as spiritual. It is also the same as psychological. While mental deals with the known, spiritual deals with the unknown. Spiritual weakness manifests as mental weakness. Lack of creativity and innovation are manifested symptoms of this. Those that are mentally weak cannot produce anything mentally. And is it not true that those who cannot produce mentally also cannot produce products, services of modern convenience? Mental, spiritual weakness always leads to stagnation, retrogression, subjugation. Faithfully defending weakness does not produce strength. Those who have lost the ability to tell the difference between truth and lies will forever be weak. Truth always depart from those who, because of selfishness, continue to defend delusion (false beliefs and outright lies) even when it is clear that they are wrong. Acceptance of truth is the antidote for delusion. It is a prerequisite for growth, for progress.

CHAPTER 11

OF CONTENTMENT AND FULFILLMENT

"Happiness is when what you think, what you say, and what you do are in harmony." Mahatma Gandhi

Presently, I always wake up every morning, with a smile, with the feeling that I do not need anything. And that feeling is not because I have everything. I do not. But I am content with what I have. I crave for nothing anymore. I feel fulfilled, despite the state of affairs in Nigeria. I feel satisfied, even though there was recession in the land, coupled with a biting inflation that is making the price of essential commodities skyrocketing every day. I feel so complete albeit I have been unable to have all my children under one roof. I feel peace inside me, around me. I have love in my heart, in my life. If I never have more than this in life, I will still die smiling, laughing, and knowing that I have lived a fulfilled life, with a feeling of completeness.

The juice of joy inside my belly is enough for an elephant to dance the jig.

I now live in a self-created cocoon. In my cocoon, there is joy. There is love. And there is peace. There is no undue financial burden in my cocoon. You all remember I do not celebrate anything, right? I have mastered the art of living within the confine of my meager means. Anyone bringing strife and discord and problems is not welcome in my cocoon. Anyone bringing undue financial burden born out of penchant for extraneous appetites is definitely not welcome. In my cocoon, there is always light, light in all its meaning. And there is this marvelous contentment born out of jettisoning of extraneous appetites. In my cocoon, I get the same feeling you get from jetting out of Lagos after dinner, having breakfast and shopping in Dubai, then proceeding to America to party with family and friends.

Simply put, I have mastered the art of enjoying the simplest pleasures that life has to offer. I have heard some people calling this luck. Hmmmm, luck ko, luck ni. This is the result of many years of prudent planning, of rearrangement of thoughts and priorities, of washing my hands clean of all illegality and corruption.

Now, I live in my cocoon, with clean hands, without rancor, without malice, laughing, loving, and living.

My contentment is not unconnected with my conviction that I have always, and I will always; reap what I sow, good or bad, big or small. I pity those who do not reap what they sow. In my opinion that is akin to someone working for months without getting paid.

My ability to deal with adversity with equanimity is also not unconnected with my conviction of sowing and reaping. If I am reaping a sour harvest as consequences of bad sowing, why waver, why wobble? Why not just calmly adjust the thinking, the doing that preceded the bad sowing?

The following story showcases the above concepts. Few days ago, a close friend from London sent a message to me through one of my aunties. As I was about to drive out, to go and pick up the message, one of my house guests came running out to stop me. She wanted me to transfer MTN credit to her son. Her bank mobile apps was misbehaving. I did the transfer and she gave me the cash. She then apologized for delaying me. I told her there was no reason to apologize, that the way things have been working in my life that she may have saved me from sitting inside that menacing Lagos traffic.

Her daughter and son-in-law were witnessing all this. And I explained the concept of synchronicity to all of them. "Synchronicity is a concept, first explained by psychoanalyst Carl Jung, which holds that events are "meaningful coincidences" if they occur with no causal relationship yet seem to be meaningfully related." Wikipedia. As I was about to get in my car, I saw my cook coming out from the back of the house.

Wow!

I instantly remembered that I had forgotten to take with me the food I asked her to make for me. I knew that there was no food where I was going. And I did not want to eat outside. I went back in to tell my house guests what I would have forgotten to take with me if someone had not ran out to "disturb" my initial exit from the house. That is how synchronicity works for me. Things I could not have done on my own get done by Providence, if I truly deserve them, if that is what my hand calls for, big or small, good or bad. This was what killed my impatience, my frustration, and my disappointment. This is where my peace of mind, my joy spring from. I think what synchronicity is to me is what "grace" is to some religious people. Those who feel it not just believe it, know it.

This is the reason why I must not, I cannot depart from the path of continually striving to do the right things the right way, if not in all things, in most things, if not at all times, most of the time.

CHAPTER 12
OF ENLIGHTENMENT AND EXCELLENCE

Enlightenment, as used in this chapter, means "insight or awakening to the true nature of reality." And, the acceleration of intuition will ultimately lead to enlightenment. Excellence, then, is the logical consequence of this enlightenment.

Let us get something straight: Truth is truth, no matter who says it, no matter where it is found or written: Just like water is water, no matter if in a cup or in a bowl. One of the errors that I see some people making is to revere containers more than the contents. These are the people that are susceptible to delusion, the type that "God" sends to those who do not love the truth. There is power in knowing the truth. There is freedom in the effective usage of the truth. Activities pursued with the knowledge of truths ultimately produce happiness and success. Those who are interested in the truth ought to master how to test truth whenever they come in contact with it. And the three tests of truths are correspondence test, coherence test and pragmatic test. "Test All Things". I repeat, "Test All Things". Because "those who have traded the right path for error, their traffic shall produce no profit."

Every human has the potential to become enlightened, and to use that enlightenment to achieve favorable and desirable results. But potential is not actual. Yet, potential can be transformed into actual with the mastery of the input-process-output model. In order to do this, we need power. What is power? It is simply the ability to achieve. What can we do without power? Mostly nothing. Therefore understanding power is absolutely necessary. There are the types of power formulated by social psychologists John R. P. French and Bertram Raven in 1959 and 1965.

(1) Legitimate power.
(2) Reward power.
(3) Expert power.
(4) Referent power.
(5) Coercive power
(6) Informational power.
(7) Connection power.

Legitimate power is formal power. For example, if we see a policeman with a gun, we know that he has the formal power to carry the gun because he represents authority and, therefore, authorized to carry arms. Reward power is the ability to reward anyone who has done something for us. Expert power is when we possess the knowledge and skills to get some things done effectively. Coercive power is to be able to force others to do what we want them to do even if they do not want to do it. Information power is to possess timely, accurate, and pertinent information. **"Connection Power** is where a person attains influence by gaining favor or simply acquaintance with a powerful person. This **power** is all about networking."

"Productivity is never an accident. It is always the result of a commitment to excellence, intelligent planning and focused effort." Paul J. Meyer. To achieve excellent productivity, we need the right combination of powers. Without the right combination, we may suffer from "illusion of power", and achievement of objectives/goals may be elusive. And, those without appropriate types of power blame external factors for their woes. They may even believe that their family is cursed. Most of the time, the problem is "within". And our intelligence, with its intuitive component firing, can assist in, not only solving problems, but also in preempting and preventing problems. Intelligence is not just the ability to learn and understand. It is also the ability to cope with new and trying situations. The usage of intelligence can be an antidote to the prevention and resolution of most problems.

No one suffers where there is excellence. "Excellence is a talent or quality which is unusually good and so surpasses ordinary standards. It is also used as a standard of performance as measured e.g. through economic indicators. Excellence is a continuously moving target that can be pursued through actions of integrity, being frontrunner in terms of products / services provided that are reliable and safe for the intended users, meeting all obligations and continuously learning and improving in all spheres to pursue the moving target." Source ~Wikipedia. "Studies have shown that the most important way to achieve excellent performance in fields such as sport, music, professions and scholarships is to practice. Achievement of excellence in such fields commonly requires approximately 10 years of dedication, comprising about 10,000 hours of effort." Source ~Wikipedia.

A source of greatness is excellence. And excellence can be reached through the continuous refinement of innate talents, innate abilities, of which everyone possesses in one form or another. Therefore, go ahead; discover yourself, by yourself, for yourself. Go from ordinary to extraordinary. You've got it in you. Maybe? I know I have it. As an initial matter, we must begin from within. Thinking, production of thoughts, which ought to be primary, is the essence of all things produced by humans.

It is a good thing, even a smart move, to learn from other cultures, other religions. After all, no one culture, religion, has monopoly on knowledge. When smart people learn from other cultures, other religions, they integrate the pertinent, newly acquired knowledge into their own culture, into their own religion. They essentially use it to innovate, to progress, to ward off the ineffectiveness that accompanies getting stuck on using obsolete knowledge, cumbersome methods that produce backwardness, financial/political/spiritual colonization.

Consequently, they are continuously learning, continuously evolving, and therefore, forever growing. For example, bows and arrows and spears that were devastating as fighting tools at one point in history are now mere hunting tools. They have essentially been overtaken by modern weaponry, and no longer relevant in the art of war.

CONCLUSION

In my scheme of things, my philosophical contraption, which is the outgrowth of my life experience, both subjective and objective, I am the one in control of my thoughts, my actions, my inactions. However, "God" is the one in control of the consequences of my actions and inactions. And, because "God" is fair, unlike a lot of human beings, "He" always makes sure I reap what I sow, good or bad, big or small. Can you see why I keep on saying that prayer, if not coupled with doing the right things the right way, is an exercise in futility? Can you see the reason why I do not pray anymore? Yet, I continue to enjoy the simple pleasures that life has to offer. I continue to live a fulfilling and satisfying life devoid of corruption. I am one of those that are truly "saved".

"One of the purpose of meditation is to calm the mind, achieve inner peace and, eventually, reach a higher dimension, often referred to simply as being." I can authoritatively tell you that I have used meditation to calm my mind, achieve inner peace, inner joy, and continually live a fulfilling and satisfying life. That is why I continue to live, love, and laugh.

If you are only happy when good things happen, then you have neither mastered happiness nor life. Both good and bad abound in this world. And no one, I repeat, no one has a monopoly on good or bad occurrence. We all have our own share of both and only those that have mastered happiness, mastered life, can keep on bubbling both in good times and bad times. I am one of those Fortune's favorite children. Good or bad times have no effect on my inner bubble, my inner peace. My emotional equilibrium is always in place. Living, loving, laughing, with these, I am living a fulfilling, satisfying life. I will die smiling. I am as trouble-free, worry-free, and stress-free as any human that is alive can wish for.

There is indeed a verifiable link between human thoughts/actions and consequences. No one has been able to make me unhappy in the last eighteen years. If they offended me, I simply forgave them. No malice. No hard or ill feeling. No hatred. Just the juice of joy flowing through me. My stomach is sweet, always. My stomach is smiling, as usual.

There is nothing beyond satisfaction but greed. If you always need more to be satisfied when less can also be satisfying, check your greed level. It may be high. If it is, come here for a crash course in personal development and contentment. But you must pay.

This is how I discovered that there is nothing beyond satisfaction but greed. In 1987 I bought a brand new BMW. I derived so much pleasure from driving this car. The leather felt nice. The stereo, ah, the music coming from the stereo was exhilarating. Yes, everything about the car was just perfect. The maneuvering of the car testified that it was indeed the ultimate driving machine. Going home to sleep at night became difficult. I would still be found driving around at 3am in the morning. And when I did park the car, instead of going in to sleep, I would go for another spin, another thrill, another enjoyment of the ultimate machine. Simply put, it was heaven.

Years later, I bought bigger, better, more expensive cars. But I never got that paradise-like feeling I got from the BMW. Then, in the year 2000, I was at my lowest in life, in isolation, without an iota trapping of wealth, and that same feeling I got from driving the ultimate machine came back to me. In the face of obvious worldly failure, the most euphoric feeling washed all over me. The fountain of joy, the spigot of peace, that were encased within my being, began the sprinkling of their everlasting contents into my life. On that very day, I decided I would no longer feed my greed. I decided to settle at any level I find satisfaction. And, eighteen years later, I am living a contented life, devoid of greed, without corruption, with joy, with peace.

The credit for the alignment that took place in my mind eighteen years ago goes to meditation, to something that is not seen but speaks, to alignment of thoughts. And to me too, for having the discipline to act on the knowledge I derived from my meditation. Life is indeed good. But we must plan it well.

 It was that incident of eighteen years ago that made me to realize that I did not need as much as I thought I needed to be happy, to be satisfied. That was the day that most things became well with me. With, or without a lot of things, I now feel complete, happy, satisfied.
If those things come my way, fine. If they don't, fine. My equanimity will not be disturbed by my lack of certain things. Life is good, not because I have all that I want, but because I am content with what I have. That means I always cut my coat according to my fabrics.

And...

I do not envy anyone. I never had, and hopefully, I never will envy anyone. Some things that others have, I may not have. And that is okay. That is life. We all cannot have the same things. But some things I do have, others do not have also. Again, that is okay. That is life. We all cannot have the same things. I have love, plenty of it. I am always bubbling with inner peace, inner joy. I live. I laugh. And I am content with the things I have. I sow. I reap. I strictly adhere to the immutable law of cause and effect. And I do not covet my neighbors' things.

So, I advise you to live, love, laugh, and enjoy the simple pleasures that life has to offer. Life is good, but you must plan it well.

I have thrown all my frustrations into the burning furnace of contentment. I have gotten rid of grudges. Grudge is a persistent feeling of ill will or resentment resulting from a past insult. I have gotten rid of malice. Malice is the desire to harm someone; ill will. I have gotten rid of hatred. Hatred is intense dislike; hate. I have gotten rid of greed. Greed is intense and selfish desire for something, especially wealth, power, or food. And... Contentment has erupted. Contentment is a state of happiness and satisfaction. Ah ha! My contentment is not the fulfillment of all that I want, but it is the realization of how much I already have. True contentment is when our happiness comes from what we have, unattached to what we do not have.